# KEYISSUES
# Working with Parents

AMY ARNOLD AND ROXANNE RUTTER

Published 2011 by Featherstone Education
Bloomsbury Publishing plc
50 Bedford Square, London,
www.acblack.com

ISBN 978-1-4081-405-12

Printed in Great Britain by Latimer Trend and Company Ltd

This book is produced using paper that is made from wood grown
in managed, sustainable forests. It is natural, renewable and
recyclable.
The logging and manufacturing processes conform to the
environmental regulations of the country of origin.

To see our full range of titles visit **www.acblack.com**

# Contents

# Introduction

Children's emotional and physical development in their early years is rapid and underpins their future lives. A strong collaboration, or working partnership, between early years practitioners and parents can have a positive impact on a child's early life that will last a lifetime. The intention of this book is to provide early years practitioners with a variety of pathways to developing their own unique approach to working with parents and thus benefit the children in their care.

Working collaboratively with parents has always been an integral and vital part of good practice within the early years sector. Working in partnership with parents is also a key message of the current Early Years Foundation Stage guidance (2008) and Dame Tickell's review of the EYFS (2011) calls for even greater partnership between parents and carers:

> 'Where parents and carers are actively encouraged to participate confidently in their children's learning and healthy development, the outcomes for children will be at their best.'

> Tickell, C. (2011)

By upholding the belief that adults significant to each child are important, special and concerned about their child's development, we will ensure that every parent matters and therefore every child will feel the strength of that solidarity.

## Who is this book for?

This book is for all early years professionals and adults working with children in a range of settings, who are in search of ideas and motivation to support their work with parents.

Nursery and pre-school staff, along with students working towards an early years qualification, will find this book invaluable. It can be used to turn thoughts into activities or approaches that could enhance working in partnership with parents, or spark an idea for adapting current practice. This book provides a bridge between requirements and what these could look like in practice. As well as providing practitioners with some starting points and ideas for consideration, many real-life examples (or case studies) are given of how some settings establish and maintain a professional working partnership with parents.

Early Years Foundation Stage (EYFS) and Key Stage 1 (KS1) teachers, head teachers, trainee teachers and learning support assistants, will all find this book useful for contemplating potential approaches when working with parents and families.

## The importance of sharing

*'Parents and families are central to a child's well-being and practitioners should support this important relationship by sharing information and offering support to learning in the home.'*

**EYFS Statutory Framework (2008)**

This book aims to offer practitioners suggestions on how to share vital information with parents — helping them to support their child's learning and development together with being confident in their own abilities.

Important note: For ease of reading, throughout the book the word 'parents' is used as a general term, however 'parents' should be taken to include parents, carers and families. As the EYFS guidance reminds us:

*'Families are all different. Children may live with one or both parents, with other relatives or carers, with same sex parents or in an extended family.'*

**EYFS 2.2 Positive Partnerships (2008)**

## Getting to know you

Getting to know a child and their individual family takes time and effort. Friendly chats and discussions with family members and parents when children first join a setting will be an essential part of establishing who cares for, or shares the care for a child. The 'All About Me' boxes featured later in this book could be a really useful way of establishing, possibly through photographs, the different family members of each individual child.

Throughout this book there is an assumption that settings will have a welcoming environment, where posters, displays and resources demonstrate their positive attitudes to disability, and to ethnic, cultural and social diversity. Within this environment meaningful, relevant words and phrases from home languages of all the children should be displayed, and regularly added to, often with the support of parents and families. A welcoming environment includes a setting where parents can bring in buggies, where toddlers are able to explore (or perhaps be offered a basket of interesting objects to investigate) whilst their parent chats to approachable, friendly staff about their big brother or sister.

The following quote, used by Dame Tickell in her review of the EYFS, encapsulates our thinking and feelings behind the creation of *Working with Parents*:

*'A child is not a vase to be filled, but a candle to be lit.'*

**François Rabelais**

Amy Arnold and Roxanne Rutter

### References

Department for Children, Schools and Families (DCSF) (2008) *Statutory Framework for the Early Years Foundation Stage*. Nottingham: HMSO

Tickell, C. (2011) Independent report on: *The Early Years: Foundations for life, health and learning*

# Why parent partnerships?

*'Parents are children's first and most enduring educators. When parents and practitioners work together in early years settings, the results have a positive impact on children's development and learning.'*

**EYFS Framework (2008)**

Each and every setting interacts on a daily basis with parents, carers and families. The warm professional relationship between practitioners and parents can have extremely positive and lasting benefits for young children. Without the expertise that parents bring, the needs of each unique child and family can't be fully met. It is crucial that parents are valued, respected and supported in sharing their vast and expert knowledge of their individual child, family and culture.

*'Parents and other close family members are aware when children feel pleased with themselves, when they are confident or fearful and when they are truly interested. They may not be aware of how their child is prepared for early literacy and numeracy but they have invaluable and intuitive knowledge about their child's personal attributes.'*

**Dowling, M. (2010)**

To ensure that early years settings provide an environment that is supportive to each and every child's development, a clear understanding of each child's personal attributes is essential. It is parents who hold the key to unlocking this invaluable insight into each little life.

*'Parents provide a learning environment which is enduring and comprehensive. It begins even before birth, operates beyond the child's day at the setting and provides continuity as the child transfers from one setting to another.'*

**EYFS Disc 2.2 Positive Relationships**

KEY ISSUES: Working with Parents

# Sharing expertise

The different aspects of our lives are intertwined and connected - what happens in one part, for example, at home or nursery, impacts and influences other parts of our lives. Sharing expertise from across all areas of a young child's life can really enable a child to flourish and thrive.

*'Parents are experts on their own child, practitioners are experts on children's learning and development. Children usually feel more confident and positive about themselves and their learning when parents and practitioners work together in an atmosphere of mutual respect.'*

**EYFS Disc 2.2. Positive Relationships**

Without crucial information from parents, it would be far more difficult, if not at times impossible, to offer provision which amongst other things, includes:

- a stimulating environment offering explorations and learning experiences based on children's interests, passions and prior experiences

- an emotional environment that respects, supports and reassures children's developing emotions

- representation and recognition of each child's cultural, religious and ethnic background

- opportunities to cement and build on children's current development and attainments, and celebrate minor and major milestones in all areas of their lives

- an understanding of the 'holistic child'

- swift identification and action to address any additional needs

- a transition period which is planned and tailored to the needs of individual children and designed to be as smooth and seamless as possible

- an awareness of children's patterns of behaviour and fascinations from their experiences in the home and wider world.

As you will read in this book, working together with parents enhances and maximises a child's learning and development potential.

## References

DCSF, *Early Years Foundation Stage Guidance* (2008)

Dowling, M. (2010) *Young Children's Personal, Social & Emotional Development*, London, SAGE Publications. p201

# Chapter 2

# Parent partnerships within the current EYFS guidance*

*At the time of going to press, the Revised EYFS Consultation was taking place.

The important and valued role of parent's involvement in their child's learning and development is a key strand of the Early Years Foundation Stage (EYFS). This chapter highlights some of the most relevant text from both the existing EYFS guidance and Claire Tickell's report.

All practitioners have a professional duty to adhere to the statutory framework of the EYFS, of which one of the overarching aims is:

*'Creating the framework for partnership working between parents and professionals, and between all the settings that a child attends'.*

**EYFS Statutory Framework (2008)**

Parent partnership is interwoven in each of the four guiding EYFS themes:

### A Unique Child

Every child is a competent learner from birth who can be resilient, capable, confident and self-assured.

### Positive Relationships

Children learn to be strong and independent from a base of loving and secure relationships with parents and/or a key person.

### Enabling Environments

The environment plays a key role in supporting and extending children's development and learning.

### Learning and Development

Children develop and learn in different ways and at different rates and all areas of learning and development are equally important and interconnected.

Particular attention is paid to partnerships within the key theme of 'Positive Relationships'.

*'Commitments are focused around respect; partnership with parents; supporting learning; and the role of the key person.'*

**EYFS Statutory Framework (2008)**

The time that young children spend at their setting is just a small proportion of their lives. Striving to make purposeful, supportive and genuine links with children's home lives and their wider community involvement can have a significant impact on their lifelong learning and development.

*'Over 70% of children's lives are spent, not in a setting, but with their family and the wider community. Therefore home and community must be recognised as significant learning environments in the lives of children.'*

**EYFS 2.2 Positive Relationships (CD ROM) (2008)**

Involving parents in making shared and informed decisions including determining the direction for their child's learning and how best to support their child's development offers the most conducive environment for young children's learning opportunities.

*'All parents can enhance their child's development and learning. Parents have the right to play a central role in making decisions about their child's care and education at every level.*

*Children usually feel more confident and positive about themselves and their learning when parents and practitioners work together in an atmosphere of mutual respect.'*

**EYFS 2.2 Positive Relationships (CD ROM) (2007)**

A recent report on the EYFS by Dame Clare Tickell highlights that the emphasis on 'Working with Parents', is indeed vital and is likely to be given even more emphasis in any future Early Years Guidance:

*'The EYFS calls for practitioners to work in partnership with parents and carers. However, I think that it could go further, and I am therefore recommending that a greater emphasis is given in the EYFS to the role of parents and carers as partners in their children's learning.'*

**Tickell, C. (2011)**

Throughout the chapters in this book many different practical examples, ideas and case studies will be explored and shared. It is all too easy to become fixed in routines and mindsets of 'this is what we do, we always have' especially when there are so many areas of practice to focus upon.

As Dame Tickell so rightly identifies in her review, practitioners need support and motivation to make changes and push their practice to a new level.

*'Stronger partnerships with parents and carers will only succeed if people working in the early years are knowledgeable, motivated and supported in their work, and if providers continue to ensure they meet the needs of local families.'*

Tickell, C. (2011)

Within our early years settings there are some truly amazing, thought provoking and ground breaking examples of how different teams work with parents.

*'I know that practitioners in many settings work very closely with parents and carers to good effect. This practice needs to be spread more widely and to become more consistent."*

Tickell, C. (2011)

It is greatly hoped that the emphasis and importance of stronger partnership working, which Dame Tickell has clearly identified in her review, will be a prominent part of any revision to the EYFS in the coming months and years.

### References

*Department for Children, Schools and Families* (DCSF) (2008) Statutory Framework for the Early Years Foundation Stage. Nottingham: HMSO

Tickell, C. (2011*) Independent report on: The Early Years: Foundations for life, health and learning*

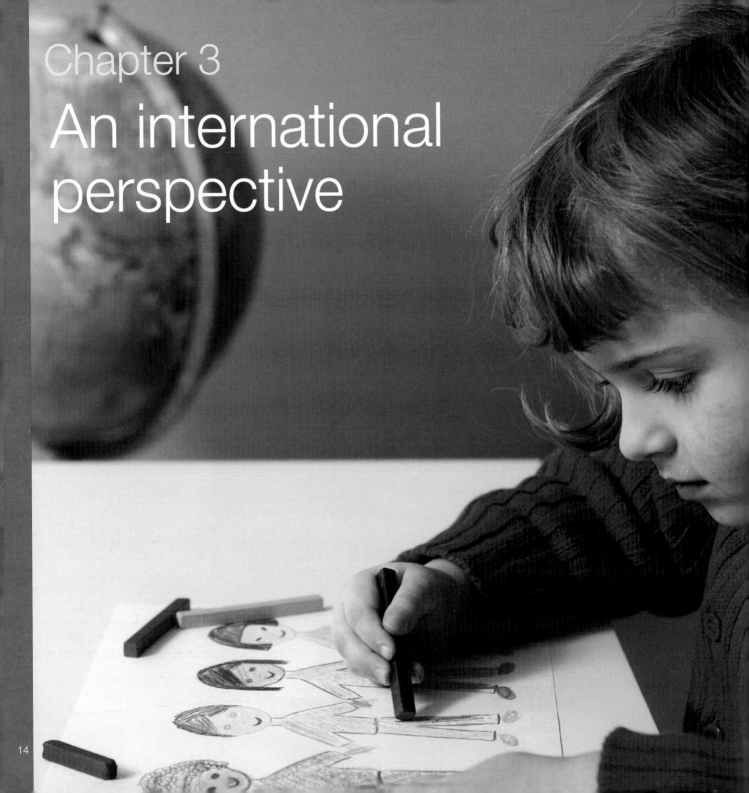

# Chapter 3
# An international perspective

This chapter will review how three influential countries, New Zealand, Italy and Sweden, approach early years education with particular attention to how parents, the home and community are valued.

## New Zealand

Te Whãriki is the curriculum for early childhood care and education in New Zealand, created in 1996.

The ECE (Early Childhood Education) states that there are two crucial principles on which Te Whãriki is based:

1.  There is scope for deliverers of childhood education to develop their own unique programme within the Te Whãriki framework to suit local cultural traditions and the environments they serve.

2.  It is equally adaptable to cater for the interests and aspirations of the child or children attending the early childhood service.

The weaving together of these factors create a robust curriculum or Whãriki (woven mat) for all to stand on.

Early childhood care in New Zealand has traditionally had to be diverse in delivery, to cater for the different communities it serves. Te Whãriki was developed to regulate the diverse approaches yet also provide stability and celebrate cultural diversity. Each community to which a child belongs, whether it is a family home or an early childhood setting outside the home, provides opportunities for new learning to be fostered:

> '..for children to reflect on alternative ways of doing things; make connections across time and place; establish different kinds of relationships; and encounter different points of view.'

(www.minedu.govt.nz)

These experiences enrich children's lives and provide them with the knowledge, skills, and dispositions they need to tackle new challenges.

The Te Whãriki curriculum aims to empower children and is based on the following aspirations for them:

> 'To grow up as competent and confident learners and communicators, healthy in mind, body, and spirit, secure in their sense of belonging and in the knowledge that they make a valued contribution to society.'

(www.minedu.govt.nz)

With society and diversity so central to its core principles, it forces providers into a culture of valuing home, and using the home as a starting point to create further learning.

The New Zealand system has heavily influenced the publication of our own EYFS. Valuing the starting point from which children come is a fundamental aspect to any early years education. Children are seen as being far from an empty vessel in which we fill them with knowledge. By contrast they are often bursting with ideas, passions and interests which if we can tune into, will release powerful and potent learning. What Te Whãriki teaches us is to value the diversity of children who enter our settings. Not just in a cultural sense, but the everyday diversity. Those unique individuals that walk through your door all have something that's definitely worth celebrating. Equally, every cohort will be different as each combination of children will produce different dynamics. It is this celebration of 'weaving individuals to become one' that we must celebrate.

# Italy

Another well documented approach to early years education is that found in a small city in Northern Italy called Reggio Emilia. It places great importance on services to the community and family. Their education system was founded after World War II by the city families who wanted to create a better life for their children after the suffering and devastation of the war. It is fundamentally an education system built on the needs of parents.

The Reggio Emilia approach to early education is committed to the creation of conditions for learning that will enhance and facilitate children's construction of their powers of thinking:

> '...through the synthesis of all the expressive, communicative and cognitive languages'

> **Edwards, Gandini and Forman (1993)**

Central to the whole approach is the concept of the child as a subject of rights and as a competent, active learner, continuously building and testing theories about themselves and the world around them.

A motto of the city for many years has been

> 'Investment in children is a fundamental cultural and social investment'

> **Thornton, L and Brunton, P (2007)**

> 'The Italian Education department allocates as much as 40% of the municipal budget to education. The sustained commitment to parent and community participation reflects the philosophy behind the city's schools as a system of relations between children, teachers, parents and the community where the school is located '...This would push our schools towards teaching without learning'

> **Malaguzzi, in Edwards et al (1993)**

Distinct pedagogical features have emerged in the Reggio Emilia approach. These include:

- an emphasis on expression and children's utilisation of multiple symbolic languages

- the development of long-term projects as contexts for children's and teachers' learning and research

- careful attention to the role of the environment as it supports relationships among the three protagonists—teacher, parent, child.

In the Reggio Emilia approach, Thornton, L and Brunton, P (2007) describe how young children are encouraged to explore their understanding of their experiences through different modes of expression considered natural to them. These 'hundred languages of children': words, gestures, discussion, mime, movement, drawing, painting, constructions, sculpture, shadow play, mirror play, drama, music and the environment, play a big part in the Reggio approach. Children are encouraged to access projects and learning (as they would at home) and parents are expected to be actively involved in the life of an early years setting and in return their opinions are respected by staff.

Having a respect for parents that runs throughout the setting is crucial for success. The Reggio approach can teach us that developing a reflective practice and valuing the contribution of parents will improve the quality of our settings and the care of our children.

# Sweden

The final approach to consider is from the Swedish curriculum. Similar to the Italian, New Zealand and British systems, there are five groups of goals that each early years centre should aim to achieve:

1.  Norms and values

2.  Development and learning

3.  Influence of the child

4.  Pre-school and home

5.  Cooperation between the pre-school class, the school and the leisure time centre

The Swedish pre-school is characterised by a pedagogical approach where care, nurturing and learning together form a coherent whole. Related to the formulation of learning goals are life skills. These correspond to qualities such as cooperative skills, responsibility, initiative, flexibility, reflectivity, active attitudes, communicative skills, problem solving skills, critical stance, creativity, as well as an ability to 'learn to learn'.

Wagner J. et al. (2006) describes the Swedish model as centring round the ideal of children being deeply involved in their own social world. Children's social development presupposes that they, according to age and capabilities, are given growing responsibility for their own actions and for the environment in pre-school. The needs and interests the children themselves express provide the foundation for shaping the environment and planning pedagogical activities. For this reason, pre-school should ensure that children develop the ability to express their own thoughts and views and thus have the opportunity to influence their own situation, develop the ability to understand and act in accordance with democratic principles by participating in different kinds of cooperation and decision making.

Wagner describes this type of risk taking and decision making based on observations:

*'...toddlers climbing a rappelling wall, using a fork to eat spaghetti with some success and skiing nimbly down a Norwegian mountain side.... 10 toddlers all under three, milling about on an underground platform in their snowsuits, waiting for a train headed to the forest ... teachers are nearby, but they do not hover or admonish the children to stay away from the edge... cutting apples with a paring knife, hanging by their knees from a tree branch while their class mates use a real saw and a power drill to construct a fort.'*

**Wagner J, & Einassdottir, J (2006)**

Wagner paints a picture of a setting where children are exposed to real and challenging experiences, and where school and home are mirror images of the other. Practitioners are allowed to educate children to be risk takers in the real world.

The influence of home and the celebration of teaching children through real life experiences strikes a chord for most practitioners. Children learn best through meaningful, rich experiences. Learning physically sticks when they experience it. The wiring of our brains physically changes when we are engaged in a meaningful activity.

The impact of developing links with parents and mirroring home life in your setting is incredible.

A key idea in all three international perspectives is a non-institutionalised approach to pre-school life. The early years setting should aim to be an environment that is reminiscent of home, with freedoms and flexibilities, where children feel like they are champions in learning.

Of course, this type of philosophy requires support from a higher level, both locally and nationally. Our education system is built on our cultural history and the experiences of previous generations. It would be unrealistic to think that we can create a perfect utopia for our education system. We operate within the boundaries of our education system and the wider limitations. We often feel that we just can't do what we know is right, placing too many obstacles in our way and inhibiting our development of a good setting.

However, learning from countries who have tried these models, with results that show academic success in later life, should inspire us to begin to adapt our practice, to try new things and to step outside our 'safe model'.

Whilst taking inspiration from the work of the educators in these countries it is important not to lose sight of the exciting, ground breaking and outstanding practice that can be seen in our own settings. Developing links within our own communities, with pre-schools, nurseries, schools and families is possibly one of the best ways we can foster a community of partnership.

## References

*Final report to the Ministry of Education*. Wellington: New Zealand Council for Educational Research. www.minedu.govt.nz

*Te Whäriki: New Zealand's Early Childhood Curriculum Document in Theory and Practice*. Wellington: New Zealand Council for Education Research. www.educate.ece.govt.nz

Edwards, C, Gandini, L, & Forman, G. (red.) (1993) *The Hundred Languages of Children. The Reggio Emilia Approach to Early Childhood Education.* Norwood, New Jersey: Ablex Publishing Corporation.

Thornton, L and Brunton, P (2007) *Bringing the Reggio Approach to your Early Years Practice.* Routldege Publishers

Einassdottir, J and Wagner, J (2006) *Nordic Childhoods and Early Education.* Information Age Publishing

# Chapter 4
## Working together to nurture growing brains

Research studies from the world of neuroscience can provide us with a greater understanding of how young brains 'work' and develop. In turn, this knowledge can be used to make a positive impact on many areas of our practice, including working with parents.

In recent years many books have made the findings from the complex and specialist world of neuroscience accessible and relevant to a wide range of audiences, including early years practitioners and parents. The combination of a basic understanding of the science behind children's emotions and behaviour with the skills and expertise of early years practitioners can help to nurture and support children.

A very basic understanding of the chemical reactions that occur in the brain during different experiences, either stressful or joyful, can help practitioners to sensitively support children (and parents) with the huge emotions and rush of feelings they may experience.

> *'Children who are encouraged to feel free to express their ideas and their feelings, such as joy, sadness, frustration and fear, can develop strategies to cope with new, challenging or stressful situations'*

**EYFS (2008)**

## Stressful experiences

Our bodies respond to stressful situations or experiences in many ways. One way is by releasing cortisol (stress hormone) and adrenalin into the brain.

> *'If we perceive the event as a disaster, the neurotransmitter adrenalin is released and the mind/ body responds with a series of survival-oriented reactions. With increased adrenalin we also produce the neurotransmitter cortisol which decreases our ability to learn and remember.'*

**Hannaford, C, (1995)**

### Separation anxiety

Often when a young child begins pre-school, playgroup or nursery it is their first experience of being away from a parent or family member. This major transition needs careful planning and managing, along with a flexible approach, dependent on the needs of each unique child.

> *'When your baby reaches six to eight months of age, separation anxiety starts to kick in and often continues in some form until she is well over five years old.'*

**Sunderland, M. (2007)**

Prior to a separation, recognised successful 'transition activities' include: home visits, the child and parent spending 'settling time' together at the setting, photo books of the setting shared at home and the child's first activities within the setting devised to be in line with their interests.

There will be times when a child experiences intense and overwhelming emotions when their parent leaves. Respecting these emotions and dealing with them in a warm, caring and supportive manner will support children's long term emotional development.

*'One study of nursery school children showed that it was not the mother's absence in itself that increased stress hormones such as cortisol, but the absence of an adult figure who was responsive and alert to their states moment by moment.'*

Dettling et al. 2000; from Gerhardt, S. (2010)

Listening to and understanding both parents and children's responses, views and anxieties to separation is essential for supporting and planning for transition and separation.

Through ample settling time and an understanding triangular partnership between parent, child and setting, a prepared and familiar path, leading to separation, can be laid together.

Empowering parents to share the importance of settling time with their employers and to seek flexibility, for this short transition period, could really help to reduce a parent's stress. It can prevent the feeling of pressure to rush out of the door, leaving their child in a state of distress in the setting, often resulting in parents being emotionally unsettled, anxious or worried when they arrive at work.

Encouraging parents to give their child a cuddle before they leave could help to reduce the flood of cortisol in the brain, as Margot Sunderland describes 'Hold him really close. This will activate opioids in his brain and will make him feel calmer. It also means that he "finds" you before he "loses" you.':

*'Holding and soothing will bring down her cortisol levels and activate a more positive chemistry in her brain*

Sunderland, M. (2007)

The role of the Key Worker is crucial in recognising the child's needs and understanding how best to support individual children through the tough feelings of separation. Strategies to reduce stress and cortisol levels may be different for each child. For example some children may calm down quicker with a cuddle or a

story whilst others may need distracting with the opportunity to do a very important job, such as feeding a pet, preparing a snack or unlocking the shed to get the bikes out. For others, a small photo book of pictures from home showing pets or family members can help a child to feel that home is still present in their setting.

However, what is vital is that all children have support from a warm, caring and understanding adult who acknowledges and respects their feelings and helps them to deal with these feelings.

*'What a small child needs is an adult who is emotionally available and tuned in enough to help regulate his states.'*

Gerhardt, S. (2010)

*'When a child is not helped enough with his intense feelings, the alarm systems in his lower brain can be over-active in later life'*

Sunderland, M. (2007)

Goleman (1996) reminds us 'Critical experiences include how dependable and responsive to the child's needs parents are, the opportunities and guidance a child has in learning how to handle her own distress and control impulse, and practice in empathy'.

Acknowledging a parent's anxieties by a phone call, email or text message once their child has settled will offer reassurance, and reduce a parent's own cortisol levels if they have left feeling stressed, and will certainly help towards building a positive partnership. When a parent comes to collect their child, giving them a photograph showing their child busily engaged during their time with you, will confirm to the parent that their child was not upset for the whole session! A photograph would also provide a wonderful starting point for a chat about their child's time at nursery.

## Overwhelming joy and euphoria

Just as stressful experiences cause a chemical rush in the brain, so too do happy and joyful experiences.

*'Opioids are brain chemicals with many functions, one is to relieve pain. However, opioids also give us a general sense of well-being… Dopamine is a brain stimulant that gives us motivation and drive.'*

Sunderland, M. (2007)

When these chemicals are released, a young child can sometimes feel overwhelmed and perhaps confused - they may be unsure how to react, of whether it is ok to let go and relish in the immense feelings of joy - or they make just feel out of control or in a state of excited bliss!

There are a variety of strategies, including stories and the use of puppets (see page 55), that you can use to help children to understand and express their feelings.

*'Intense feelings of joy produce lovely chemicals in the brain but also high levels of bodily arousal and activation of stress chemicals.'*

Sunderland, M. (2007)

*'When children are not helped with the 'stress' of joy, they can be frightened of the bodily arousal of excitement in later life.'*

Sunderland, M. (2007)

Here are some other strategies to help children to manage and express their emotions:

- Mirror back a child's facial expression and share in the feelings of joy or amazement to reassure them that it is OK to feel like this and they can enjoy it.

- Share with parents examples of when a child has experienced joy and sheer delight during their time with you. This provides the opportunity for parents to chat about the child's exciting times and feelings and further support the development of their emotions.

*'Children, like adults are more likely to talk about things that affect them with people who show that they are genuinely interested, who are prepared to give time to listen and who reciprocate with some of their experiences. Children's feelings will be stirred by sensory experiences such as listening to music, looking at and touching beautiful things, tasting and smelling. If they can talk about their reactions to these positive experiences, it will alert them to recognise similar feelings on another occasion.'*

**Dowling, M. (2010)**

- A photograph of a child enjoying the magic of the parachute lifting into the air and the sensory feel of it landing on them, or a simple egg shaped piece of paper with a message 'Ask me all about the chicks hatching!' could stimulate the sharing between parent and child of these wonderful sensory events and the feelings that were experienced.

Involving parents in understanding some of the big feelings and emotions their child may have experienced during their time away from home can help parents to be ready to acknowledge and reassure should they experience similar feelings at home or wish to chat about their day.

Share with parents the importance of recognising and reassuring children when they experience a rush of emotions and flood of chemicals.

### References

Department for Chidren, Schools and Families (DCSF) (2008) *Statutory Framework for the Early Years Foundation Stage.* Nottingham: HMSO

Gerhardt, S. *Why Love Matters* (2010) Routledge

Goleman,D. *Emotional Intelligence*, (1996) Bloomsbury, London

Hannaford, C. *Why learning is not all in your head*, (1995) Great Ocean Publishers, U.S.

Sunderland, M. *What every parent needs to know*, (The Science of Parenting) (2007) DK, London

# Chapter 5
# Sharing Experiences

# Special days

Sharing experiences in partnership with the child, setting, home, and community can offer great potential for maximizing learning opportunities, along with building new skills, interest groups and raising aspirations. They can also make some great memories for everyone involved!

Settings can play a key role in facilitating opportunities and experiences, whilst bringing parents together and creating valuable time to talk informally, face-to-face in a relaxed, non-structured environment.

> *'It is the power of face-to-face conversation, building relationships based on trust and integrity that makes the biggest difference. All of this takes time, commitment and patience. Real and deep listening, responding to what parents say and keeping promises are key factors in building the trust that seems to underpin a genuine partnership.'*

**NCSL (2010)**

The type and range of opportunities for children and parents to get together in a relaxed environment will be dependent on each setting's unique families and communities.

A few simple ideas on the following pages could offer a starting point for engaging with and creating shared experiences with parents and families.

## Meeting at the local park, farm or woods

This could be organized in many different ways. Some of the approaches which have worked well for settings include: Meeting at the park on a Saturday morning or weekday late afternoon (around 4pm). Parents and other family members (including grandparents) come along to spend the morning in the park or perhaps come and collect their child from the park instead of the setting. Of course, each setting has their own set of logistics to make it work for them in their area. Whilst it could seem like a great deal of juggling and organizing, the long lasting benefits could be enormous.

## A visit to the setting in the dark for a bedtime story!

(It really doesn't have to be too late, especially after the clocks have gone back.) Children, parents, siblings and their favourite bedtime companion, perhaps teddy or snuggle cat, come back to the setting in their pyjamas all ready for their bedtime story! With duvets, blankets or throws for the children to sit on or under, along with a cosy lamp or dim lighting, children can snuggle down for their bedtime story with their familiar practitioner, who is of course, also in their pyjamas! Amazed to see friends in their pyjamas, excited at being in their familiar setting in a new and special way, children can experience stories differently too! With a hushed voice and teddy bear, sleepy bedtime stories and tales just demand to be shared!

Perfect bedtime stories include: *Husherbye* by John Burningham, *Sleep Tight Little Bear* or *Can't You Sleep Little Bear?* both by Martin Waddell or *My Blanket Is Blue* by Hilda Offen. In this way you can create a magical, snoozy storytime – rich with the language of bedtime and sleep in a meaningful shared experience. Perhaps, in a separate area, parents can enjoy a hot chocolate and the opportunity to talk to other parents, without the pressure of dropping off or picking up children! Practitioners can informally chat with parents, building relationships, beginning to understand one another - making links to strengthen and support children's learning and development. Of course, parents could also be part of the magical bedtime stories!

## Family days out

As the case study of Sandcastles Playschool (see page 52) demonstrates, family days out can be a brilliant opportunity for sharing experiences. Parents will be supported as staff are on hand to assist, wherever needed.

Travel beyond the immediate neighbourhood widens children's awareness of their local area and the wider world, whilst providing a wonderful opportunity for discussion and exploration. Taking lots of photographs will provide a stimulus for revisiting, reflecting and recounting their experience back at Nursery.

A bus trip and a packed lunch are sure-fire winners, irrespective of the distance travelled or final destination!

# Sharing everyday tasks

Planning for children to have access to hands-on 'homely' activities (such as gardening, cooking, sewing or cleaning) within the setting, can lead to powerful learning experiences.

Homely activities such as washing up, cooking, hanging out washing, gardening (from yoghurt pots to vegetable plots) or cleaning can provide wonderful contexts for active learning and problem solving: I wonder how we could clean the buckets? How many buns will we need for the fairies' picnic?

Familiar activities could also provide a starting point for linking with a young child's home environment; an opportunity to observe, listen and note if children make connections with their home environments.

Actively involving children in everyday activities offers endless, invaluable opportunities for learning essential life skills.

Tell me and I'll forget

Show me and I may remember

Include me and I'll understand

**Chinese proverb**

It is important for the practitioner to reassure parents that children don't need hours of one to one time or 'special' activities or resources in order to learn. Explain to them that it's actually the little things such as involving children in everyday tasks that can make a big difference to the child's learning and their growing relationship with their child. Valuing and respecting the learning which children and parents experience together is crucial in building and maintaining a working parent partnership.

By linking homely activities within the setting, you will provide the best conditions for supporting and strengthening children's learning and development. Give ample opportunity for children to play with the home learning activities during their time in the setting, ensuring equality for all children and the chance to share, consolidate and talk about their learning at home.

As a starting point, provide a resource as a hook for parents to have a way in, to alleviate their fears. Parents could well be thinking 'Oh what does the school want?' or 'I don't know how you learn when I'm cleaning!'. Perhaps initiate an open ended focus, changing each month, linked to children's explorations at home. Here are some ideas:

## Learning in the bathroom

Make and provide parents with bath-shaped blank mini books; with a little information on the inside cover highlighting just one or two possibilities for learning in the bathroom (see the example below for some ideas).

Within the setting, provide opportunities for children to explore and play with bathroom resources such as baby baths, ducks, bubbles, face cloths and empty bottles and give them the chance to share their findings or make links with their explorations at home.

Display any of the bath books returned from home at child height along with bathroom products, bath toys, towels or sponges. These could stimulate children to share and discuss their findings whilst having the chance to listen to and find out what their friends have been learning about in their bathrooms!

We know what an eager little learner your child is! We would love you to share with us the fabulous learning that you do at home...in the bathroom! Maybe...

- You have fun investigating the bubbles! What do the bubbles do? What do you find out? Where do the bubbles go?

- Your child has been busy testing out things which float and sink. What happened?

- Rhyme time! Rub a dub dub, 5 little ducks... What songs have you been singing in the bath?

- Pouring, filling, looking at labels... Where will bathroom fun lead you?

We can't wait to see what you have been busy doing in the bathroom!

# Learning through cooking

Following a similar format to Learning in the bathroom, send home a spoon-shaped snippet of information (example shown) along with two or three paper templates of maybe an apron or mixing bowl.

Chat informally with children and parents about daily life occurrences such as, 'What did you have for breakfast?' This gives you a chance to capture parents' and children's comments and use them to plan activities based on children's experiences. 'How could we find out why Rasheed's rice krispies went snap, crackle and pop?' This kind of informal chat could lead to inviting parents in to share their skills and expertise by demonstrating and cooking with the children. What a wonderful opportunity to find out about the lives and cultures of others! Traditional Polish cooking, Indian chapattis, Somalian snacks, or the fragrant spices of Bangladeshi dishes could fill the air and lead to a learning journey, specific to each individual group and setting.

Celebrate children's learning through cooking by bringing together home and setting discoveries and creations in a large communal book full of photographs, the shaped papers from home and any recipes are sure to be a popular shared read in the book area!

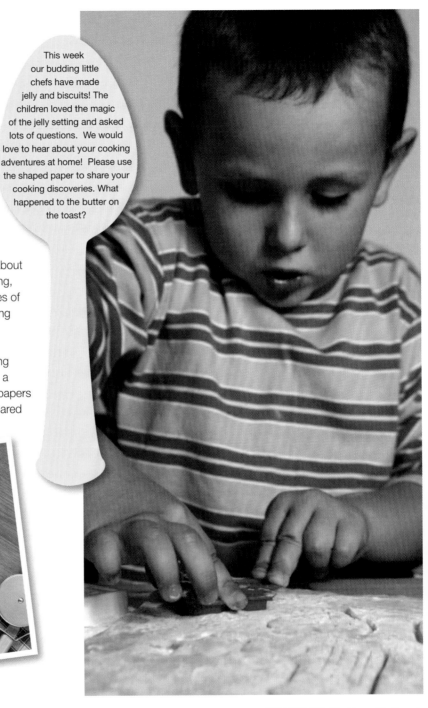

This week our budding little chefs have made jelly and biscuits! The children loved the magic of the jelly setting and asked lots of questions. We would love to hear about your cooking adventures at home! Please use the shaped paper to share your cooking discoveries. What happened to the butter on the toast?

## Learning through growing

Give each child an empty yoghurt pot, a sandwich bag of compost and a seed to take home with a little note attached: 'I wonder what will happen?'

Ask parents to help their child to complete a 'My Seed Diary' that records changes to the seed as it grows and the comments their child makes, e.g. 'I see a green bit' or 'It needs water'.

By planting the same seeds in the setting, children can compare the growth of their seed at home with those at the setting. They may share top tips for looking after the seed. As knowledge and experiences transfer between home and school, learning and development can be reinforced, cemented and shared between the key people in a young child's life.

The list of opportunities for sharing experiences between home and school in a similar style to the three examples provided are ongoing and endless and could include:

## Learning through cleaning

Perhaps each child could take a cleaning cloth home and record what they did with it: 'With my cloth I...' What a varied response this could generate! Wonderful and varied tales and adventures could stimulate talk and discussion about children's lives away from the setting.

## Learning through trips I make

Trips to school, to auntie's or to the doctor.... Children's lives can be quite busy! Encourage children to report (through talk or mark making) things they see or discover: 'On the way to school I found out that when you touch a snail he goes back into his shell!'

## Learning through me!

A 'me' paper chain of daily new experiences and achievements, made at the setting and then continued at home, could enable the sharing of key learning information, such as: 'I counted 4 buttons on my top', 'Daisy matched up all her spotty socks' or 'I made hand prints with paint and counted my fingers up to 5'.

## Learning through celebrating

Perhaps a disposable camera could be sent home when children have a celebration? Weddings, christenings or birthdays could all be captured and shared. Discussing people, clothes, food, similarities and differences are so much more meaningful when the photographs are real and relevant to their own lives!

## Learning through shopping

Set up a simple shop in your setting with signs and posters on the wall to enable children to model and share their individual experiences of shopping, 'How many items does it take for the basket to become too heavy to carry?' 'Did you spot any letters from your name on the signs or posters?' 'Why does the conveyer belt stop?'

Displaying items and artefacts that represent children's time and lives away from the setting, and the people who are important to them, offers a gentle, familiar, safe talking point. There is no right or wrong, children know all about their own items and these can act as props to support children talking about their lives. The items may be linked to a theme, children's interests or follow on from learning and investigating in the setting. Each setting will have their own ideas about what items could represent their unique children's lives at home, they may include:

- My favourite story (make sure a copy is available)

- A photo of me as a baby or something from when I was little

- Photographs of my family. Send disposable cameras home with the child home along with a note: 'Please take photographs of your family members!'

- Sending home a small ball of air drying clay, in a sandwich bag with a little label: 'You can choose to make anything at all, just leave it in the air to dry and bring back next Friday!' What fun! The variety will be astounding – small pots with decorations, models of favourite footballers, animals, initials from names. The list is endless and it may uncover a hidden skill of a parent which could be shared in school!

# Importance of the home learning environment

The EPPE (Effective Provision of Pre-school Education) Project identified a link between children's home learning environments (HLE) and their development in specific areas.

> *'The original EPPE study followed children to the end of Key Stage 1 (age 7). It explored the impact of pre-school on children's cognitive and social/behavioural outcomes, as well as other important background factors (family and home learning environment)'*

**http://eppe.ioe.ac.uk/eppe**

> *'The quality of the home learning environment (activities with children providing learning opportunities e.g. teaching songs and nursery rhymes) promoted intellectual and social development in all children.'*

**http://eppe.ioe.ac.uk/eppe**

All parents should be aware of the impact they have on their child's learning and to feel secure and confident that all the things they do and the precious time and energy they invest, are hugely important for their child's development, both current and future.

Embrace the findings of the EPPE project and actively seek to involve parents in all areas of life at your setting. Here are some ideas to get you started:

- Send home the words to favourite songs and rhymes, then invite parents in ten minutes earlier than the allocated collection time so they can hear and be part of the singing - a wonderful way to start the week on a Monday and end the week on a Friday.

- Print out recipe cards (of course designed and illustrated by the children!) and send home along with tasters of the creations made. It may inspire parents to try it out at home!

- Find out what songs parents liked as children. Could they teach the group a new song or rhyme? Or send in the words? Celebrate and share the rich and diverse experiences children have at home.

KEY ISSUES: Working with Parents

By the end of Key Stage 1 the impact of children's early home learning environment was still exceptionally strong as the following extract from 'EPPE Project: The findings from pre-school till the end of Key Stage 1' demonstrates:

*'What parents and carers do makes a real difference to young children's development. The EPPE project developed an index to measure the quality of the Home Learning Environment (HLE). There are a range of activities that parents undertake with pre-school children which have a positive effect on their development. For example, reading with the child, teaching songs and nursery rhymes, painting and drawing, playing with letters and numbers, visiting the library, teaching the alphabet and numbers, taking children on visits and creating regular opportunities for them to play with their friends at home, were all associated with higher intellectual and social/behavioural scores. These activities could also be viewed as 'protective' factors in reducing the incidence of SEN because children whose parents engaged regularly in home learning activities were less likely to be at risk for special educational needs. The home learning environment was only moderately associated with parents' educational or occupational level and was more strongly associated with children's intellectual and social development than either parental education or occupation. In other words what parents do with their children is more important than who parents are.'*

**http://eppe.ioe.ac.uk/eppe**

The EPPE project continued tracking the same children through to the age of 10 (Year 5) and the effects of their home learning environment in the pre-school years was still evident: 'Child, family and early HLE factors remain important influences on children's social/behavioural development at age 10, especially for 'hyperactivity' and 'self-regulation'.

If ever practitioners feel disheartened, weary or lacking motivation to use each and every day as an opportunity to build and strengthen links with parents, then the following two findings of the EPPE 3-11 project should highlight just how vital the work of Early Years Practitioners really is:

*'As children move through primary school, we would expect pre-school influences to lose some of their potency, or to be masked by the effects of primary schools attended. Nevertheless, significant pre-school effects are still evident in children's social behaviour five years into primary education.*

*Overall a child who has a good Home Learning Environment (HLE) in the early years, a high quality pre-school and who goes on to attend a medium or high academically effective primary school is more likely to show improved social/behavioural outcomes compared with children that have two, one or none of these experiences.'*

http://eppe.ioe.ac.uk/eppe3-11

Everyday makes a difference. Working to ensure young children have magical, memorable and rich opportunities for learning, whilst striving to build and maintain a shared and valued partnership with parents, will have significant, life enhancing effects for the children, and in turn the next generation of adults.

> ### References
> http://eppe.ioe.ac.uk/eppe

# Recording experiences

Depending on the type of setting you work in, how long the children are with you and where children move on to next, could determine just how the '101 project' is set up and how each experience is shared and celebrated. There are so many ways that the experiences could be catalogued, stored and shared between home, school and community life. Just two approaches are detailed below:

## My passport

Each child has a 'passport' created for them, which is transferred and shared between home and school. It could be a notebook, booklet, small file, folder – as long as it has space for cuttings, tickets, stamps, photographs and can be added to over time or a 'Part two' created.

One primary school divided the experiences into different age groups from Nursery to Year 2 (in response to parents' suggestions for 'structure'). A full list of the 101 experiences was always in the back of the passport so any opportunity could be maximised, if for example there was snowy weather or children visited a new place. Of course, the experiences should be repeated, whatever year group, as this is how children learn and master their skills by building upon previous experiences — refining, enhancing, transferring and applying new skills. How wonderful to record what Harry's sandcastle looks like in Nursery, Reception, Year One and Year Two! As turrets grow and detail becomes more sophisticated, knowledge of buildings and castles appears, moats are added and flags made - a perfect opportunity for assessment.

If children's play and learning lead to building a den, growing potatoes or any other identified childhood experience during their time away from home, this can be recorded in their passport, along with photographs and annotated with the children's thoughts and ideas: 'The den was really dark!', 'We had to keep covering the potatoes when they grew'.

Parents could support their child in recording experiences - using photographs, attaching pine needles from the woods and such like to capture their explorations!

As passports flow backwards and forwards from home and school, they become really precious and children just love sharing with their group the new experiences they encounter both in and out of their home!

Involving the community could extend and add a new dimension to children's experiences, as well as developing and extending their knowledge and awareness of the immediate and wider community. Perhaps the local library could create mini certificates or stamp passports as children take out and return books or maybe the local swimming pool could offer one free swimming session or a discount from a set of lessons or sessions?

Approaching local community groups and sharing aims of the project could well lead to some wonderful opportunities for rich and shared experiences.

# Going Large!

Another setting approached the project in a different way, their circumstances were different and children moved onto different settings after a year or two with them.

Together practitioners created a huge display in a covered area outside, next to the door where parents enter the building. Experiences were displayed on large balloon shaped card, around 15 at a time, with the title: 'Have you.......'

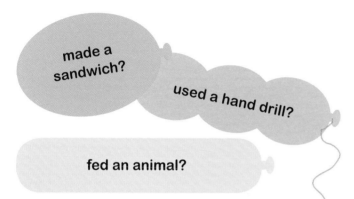

made a sandwich?

used a hand drill?

fed an animal?

Photographs or pieces of paper with the details of a child's achievements were attached to the ribbon of each balloon and both parents and practitioners would contribute by adding to the display! New experiences/balloons were frequently added and previous balloons moved inside, creating a wonderful continuous display around the area, which of course allowed for children, parents and practitioners to continue adding to them.

As the children came close to moving to their new settings, the information from the balloons was transferred into each child's individual record of learning, ready for them to take onto their next setting, bursting with examples of their rich learning experiences from home and pre-school!

The balloons gave parents and practitioners an instant talking point – a brilliant way in to informally chatting about their child's experiences and achievements. By having a shared approach, parents felt comfortable identifying which experiences they would be able to provide at home and those they wanted the setting to facilitate. Lighthearted and friendly daily interactions often included

exchanges such as: 'I'll leave the mud pie making to you! But we'll make a sandwich at home'.

Parents felt their contributions were valued, but they didn't feel too pressured as they could see what experiences their child had been engaged in during their session times. The frequent and friendly conversations based on the child's experiences, and the learning which developed from them, gave practitioners a fabulous way in to discussing plans for a child's future learning.

'Amir knew straight away when he cut his sandwich that there were four pieces'. This simple sharing of information allowed Amir's key worker and his parent to discuss the next steps in Amir's learning and plan for opportunities to build upon his current achievements. It was decided that Amir's mum was going to support him at home in making sandwiches for his little brother too and counting how many there would be all together. In the setting, practitioners were going to look for Amir instantly recognising four objects in other contexts, such as wheels on a car or legs on a dinosaur to see if he was able to apply his knowledge in different situations.

# Chapter 6

## A little bit of your setting going home...

...and a little bit of home coming into your setting

Build and strengthen the links between your setting and the children's homes with the ideas in this chapter. Be inspired to empower parents with information about their children and find alternative ideas for communicating with parents.

*The family and parenting institute states that the influence from home is 'enduring, pervasive and direct'.*

**www.earlyhomelearning.org**

As we have read in earlier chapters, home learning is a valuable and vital part of early education. We should always support and value the time and support that parents can give at home and respect that parental and family contribution will have a greater impact on achievement than the quality of schooling received.

We should ensure that our attitude is switched to being helpful and supportive to parents. Our ultimate long term goal is for happy well developed children, and by working with parents and ensuring we help them as much as possible we will go a long way to achieving this.

*'The family is where we give our children roots to grow from and wings to fly.'*

**S. Palmer (2006)**

Tim Brighouse writes that all leaders, practitioners and teachers should:

*'go out of their way to arrange meetings and adjust their behaviour to make each parent (they are all different of course) feel comfortable and not unnecessarily threatened.'*

**T. Brighouse (2006)**

Home learning is our link with parents – it is the way we share our style and our methods. If we send home meaningless worksheets then we give out the message that we value a results driven style of learning, ignoring the important process that the children went through. The process is after all the most meaningful part of home learning. We want to ensure that children enjoy the journey of learning, not just to get a sticker or the best score in class. We want children to be motivated and inspired and able to work on their own and with others. The right approach to home learning will help to do this.

## Ideas to engage parents

Often families can appear to lack confidence in engaging with staff or spending time in the setting. These are the families that we must strive to support, engage and find a shared understanding — to help a little bit of the setting to go home with them.

Sue Palmer talks in her book *Toxic Childhood* about the urgency to help 'detoxify' the toxic influences today's young children can potentially be presented with:

> *'As the world moves at electronic speed and the toxic influences on the children of the poor increase, there's every chance of serious civil unrest within a generation… Just detoxifying our own children's lives isn't enough.'*

S. Palmer (2006)

There are so many ways that you can inspire children and their parents to fall in love with home learning through stimulation, encouragement, love, security, and talk. Early communication skills and strong personal and social development are the key elements from the EYFS review in 2011. The ideas presented here will stimulate early communication, mathematical development and personal, social and emotional development.

### The story box

Story boxes are amazing tools when teaching children to read. Simply, they are a small world in a shoe box.

If your setting permits, set up time, space and cheap, readily available resources (shoeboxes, glue, variety of paper, card, fabric, pipe cleaners etc.) to enable parents to come into the setting to work with their child to create their unique story box. These boxes could be sandy beaches, moon craters, dolls' houses, car tracks, jungles, castles, mountains, woodland or even a fun fair! The

possibilities are endless. Demonstrating the wonder of story boxes at a workshop for parents could lead to asking them to create, with their child, their child's fantasy world!

Once the story boxes are made, watch and listen to the storytelling that emerges. Children will create characters, settings, story beginnings, disasters, and adventures; with your help they will develop their language, imagination and their confidence as both a talker and a writer. If every other child in your setting was to make a story box, you could soon have a large number of instant story boxes to hand. Why not operate a loan system for parents to borrow each other's boxes?

As an alternative to a school reading book, perhaps a story box could go home once a week with a blank comic book for the child to fill in with their own stories. This could build and build as each child borrows the box.

### How to make a space odyssey story box

To create a space odyssey story box cut the front off a shoe box and paint the inside black. Leave it to dry then ask a keen child to splatter it with runny white paint (this makes a starry sky). Next shred lots of tissue paper or newspaper, scrunch it up in a heap and form a crater. Ask a willing child helper to cover with gluey paint (this acts as a type of paper mâché). Once dry encourage the child to add their own characters to the planet – they could make aliens out of pipe cleaners, or use a photograph of their own little monster cut to size and glued to a lolly stick.

These story boxes have been inspired by the well known early years educator, Helen Bromley. Having been fortunate enough to attend a story box workshop with Helen, it became addictive! Over the past 8 years the fun, challenge and expansion of using story boxes with children, parents and families has resulted in some amazing results! Helen's book *50 Exciting Ideas for Storyboxes* provides a plethora of ideas to get you started.

## The story sack

Story sacks are a bag (or sack) containing a collection of resources linked to a story or non-fiction theme. They can be bought from most educational suppliers but this can be expensive so why not make your own? All you need to do is choose your favourite book and gather together a variety of resources that match the book.

When children read a story with the props from a story sack, the story really comes alive!

You might be able to enlist the help of a keen parent (or grandparent) to find or make resources for a story sack, you could have one story sack in development each term. Ask parents and carers to 'look out' for key props, for example the story *Whatever Next?* by Jill Murphy is a wonderful story for turning into a story sack — a colander from the kitchen, an old cardboard box, a stuffed owl, some red wellington boots and you have your very own adventure!

As with the story boxes, you could operate a loan system for parents to borrow the story sacks. Encourage parents to share: 'What did you do?' or 'What happened?' Watch carefully — did the child begin to interpret and play with the story? When you are sending a sack home with a child you could include a disposable camera so parents can take a few snaps of their child, busy retelling, re-enacting and reading! This would build a lovely bank of ideas for using the resource for the next borrower.

## Story pebbles

Story pebbles are a wonderfully peaceful way to tell a story. Each child is given a pebble (or asked to scavenge their own over the holidays) and then asked to draw a picture on their pebble. This can be of anything they like. When the pebbles come back together a 'hotch potch' of characters will emerge and different ideas will join together.

Working in small groups or creating a large story pebble area, encourage children to use their wonderful imaginations to make up a story from the collection of stony characters.

## Living number lines

Invite children to create a resource for the classroom – a living number line.

- Provide a camera for children to take home and make a photographic number line featuring them with their number collections: my 1 cat, my 2 favourite wellington boots, my 3 brothers, my 4 best cars, my 5 sunflowers, etc. You could then print and mount this photographic number line in a book or record on a slideshow.

- Provide coloured thread or cord to tie on items from the garden or collected from a walk, e.g. 1 pine cone, 2 shells, 3 feathers, 4 green leaves, 5 stones, etc.

Living number lines provide a fantastic opportunity for children to chat with adults and other children about their number line, how they made it, who collected the items, took the photos etc. There is no right or wrong, they are the expert!

## Reading games

Families can choose their favourite book and have a go at creating a game based on the book. This will only be effective if you have sent home some examples of this first. Ask the children to take home a favourite book e.g. *Goldilocks and the Three Bears*, read the story and then make lolly stick character puppets to re-enact the story, make up a quiz about the book characters or make porridge that Goldilocks would love to eat! Give parents the opportunity to make a reading game with their child at your setting.

1 pine cone

2 shells

### Welly walk

Take the children for a walk outside and using the inspirations found on the walk send home snippets and ideas, 'Today on our Welly walk we found a snail. Can you make a snail trail with your finger? Can you make a snail book? Do you know any snail songs or rhymes? Can you move really slowly like a snail?'

# Using objects to inspire

Providing parents with an object to take away and bring back is a great way to ensure a good response from a home learning project. These home learning projects could work on a termly basis — gauge feedback from parents to determine how frequently home learning projects would work best for them. Some of the ideas below are designed so that not every child will take a specific item every week, but a rolling programme is developed. Seeing home learning as a process rather than an end product means that we value the experience of engagement.

### Seeds

At the beginning of the year give each child a seedling to take home and nurture. Perhaps the pots could have little notes or a riddle attached…. 'I may be green. I may be yellow, I can be small and I can be tall. I'm sometimes strong. Will I ever reach the sun?' The children can have a linked activity each week to update the progress of their seedling. What is happening to it? How high is it getting? What has it been eating? Where does it live?

### A disposable camera

Sending home a cheap disposable camera can be a wonderful talking point. It could be sent with a little bear in a rucksack 'Please give me a home for the night' or perhaps with a note attached to a booklet entitled 'Show us how you learn at home!' with examples of the bear helping dad in the garden, cooking with nanny, eating my Alphabetti Spaghetti, etc.

### DVDs and home videos

Lend an MP3 player to parents to take home and record children talking, singing or telling stories or provide recordable DVDs to share photographs and 'home videos'. Alternatively videos, pictures and audio files could be emailed to the setting.

### A mysterious object

Make up a collection of objects in small boxes or containers that go home for the children to investigate and discuss with their parent. How the discussion is recorded can be left open ended but provide discussion prompts and possible follow up ideas: Who does this belong to? What is it used for? Can you draw the owner? What do they want you to do with it?

## Topic starters

Linking home learning to a topic children may have been exploring within your setting can inspire and generate ideas and questions. Making the project open ended over a long period of time encourages ongoing shared learning and discovery. It is always a good idea to have a go at each home learning activity yourself as well as asking all staff in your setting to do the same. This will not only show your enthusiasm but it will set the standard, the expectation and provide a variety of ideas and different ways of interpreting a project starter.

### Topic mobiles

Mobiles are a great way to start a topic and show how much children know, for example, 'Please show us what you know about under the sea by making an 'Under the Sea' mobile'. You could start by twisting two coat hangers together and attaching dangling objects that you know are from the sea. This project can lead to a family trip to the seaside in the holidays or research at the local library.

### Mind map

Ask the children to simply tell you all that they know about a topic and what they want to find out. This reveals lots about the children's prior knowledge as well as letting parents know what the setting will be exploring. This can be done very simply with pen and paper or evolve into a 3D collage.

### Collections

Generate collections around a topic. For example, an 'Under the Sea' topic could lead to children and parents bringing in shells, collecting bottles of sand, metallic treasure, things that float, things that sink or favourite bath toys. Collections are an easy way to get children motivated as they are able to sort, transport and examine all of the objects brought in. Invite each child to bring in one item from the collection list and you will have instant display and topic resources.

## Important things to remember

- Behind every home learning project there should be a reason. Practitioners should always model their expectation for a project.

- Every home learning project should have links to the Foundation Stage Profile. The links may not always be obvious to families, so provide a learning tag with each activity. This can be a handwritten luggage label tied to the object or learning activity to show the links to the profile or development strands.

- Always make home learning relevant for children and their families. Be aware that there may be other siblings at home placing their own demands on parents' time. Where possible think of ideas that will help parents. For example, over the Christmas holiday link activities to something you know many families may be doing such as: build a snowman as tall as you, write a thank you letter to (great aunt/grandmother/uncle), collect all of the leftover wrapping paper and wrap a meringue – can you wrap carefully so it can be posted without it breaking? Children could carry out a test and wrap and post the meringues to your setting to see which ones make it without breaking!

- When planning activities think about the seasons or the wider environment to ensure appropriateness of a task.

- Some of the ideas listed above are resource heavy and dependent on parents having time. Very often working families have more and more demands placed upon them. Finding time to complete projects is difficult. The one thing that we want from families is for parents and children to spend time together, engaging in meaningful conversation and purposeful activity. For that reason the home learning projects listed above do not have a set time scale, they are designed to be long term activities that bring families together.

# Engaging parents

As discussed at the start of this chapter, the learning that happens at home is as important and meaningful as the learning that happens in the setting. Parents are the first and most enduring educators (EYFS, 2008). The role of the practitioner is to provide meaningful and inspiring experiences for parents as well as children. Ensure that your setting has a good up-to-date policy for parent partnerships — ensure that it is diverse and open to all. How do we make sure that home learning is meaningful, relevant, exciting, and valuable to the range and diversity of families in our care?

## Newsletters

Individual letters, newsletters and emails can dripfeed valuable information to help parents understand what their child is learning at the setting. Make sure that you get your communication right and include separated parents in all letters or emails. By constantly providing snippets of information on 'why we do what we do' parents are educated to do the best.

## Home learning club

Set up a home learning club to encourage reluctant or shy parents to participate in home learning activities. Provide a welcoming space, resources and hands on support to guide parents and carers with their home learning projects. Use this time to engage with parents.

## Hands on workshops

Invite parents to come along to a workshop (perhaps in the early evening) that focuses on an aspect of their child's learning. For example, you could have a phonics workshop. Set up games, resources and methods for teaching phonics in a meaningful, child centred way (letters in the water, writing small notes to a fairy queen) for the parents to look at and ask questions about. Explain to parents how and why you teach phonics and the theory behind it.

Sadly some parents are put off by the thought of going back into the classroom and with demands of work and home life, may not feel a workshop is their priority. Your marketing of these events must stimulate curiosity to come but be such that parents don't feel pressure to attend. Workshops must feel relaxed, informative and worth their time. Extras like providing cheese and wine or free resources may encourage parents to step back into school!

Too often parents have a subconscious fear from their own experiences of school days and would rather avoid having too much to do with school, only remembering negatives from their own schooling. The relationship that you have with the parents of your children will be key – if you're approachable and friendly they will be more likely to come and spend their evening with you.

## Demonstrating play

Invite parents into the setting during the day to demonstrate how you play! Have your setting arranged with interesting but simple learning environments; a sand tray with sieves and gems, a water tray with coloured water, glitter pots, bubbles and boats, a reading corner with puppets or a story sack, a small world tray set up with dinosaurs, moss and bark with mini treasure maps and pen pots.

Model how you allow a child to lead the play. In addition to this add written question prompts to each learning environment/station to help parents to participate. These sheets can be copied for parents to take home.

## Experts

Invite experts in to talk with parents. The experts could be from a variety of areas – from speech and language or behaviour management specialists to storytellers or puppeteers. Marketing an event led by a guest speaker with the promise of tips and advice is another root into accessing many different families.

# Digital communications

Fast paced advances in technology have opened the door to new or alternative methods of communicating with parents. There are very few parents without a mobile phone; this can be used as a great way for parents to receive short messages. There are many service providers who offer a simple package where messages can be sent to parents' mobile phones using a PC. Share those wonderful 'woo hoo' moments! How fantastic for a parent to receive a message whilst they are busy shopping or at work — a message to celebrate and share their child's achievements! For example 'Kian has been super busy playing with the farmyard, he has made a wonderful story with the farmer, tractor and hungry cows!' or 'Lily has zipped up her own coat AND helped her friends to zip theirs up too!' or 'Sam has been an amazing writer, ask him about his postcard for Fireman Sam!'

Making time (just a couple of minutes) to send a celebration message each day could be achievable for many settings, creating a real positive interaction between setting, child and home.

Really involve the child in sharing their success, 'Shall we send a magic message to Daddy/Mummy?' This is a real opportunity to experience firsthand how everyday technology is used, as well as building upon and cementing the friendly relationships between all. Instantly, children and their parents have something to discuss about the day and the door has been opened to stimulate talk about their activities.

When children are gathered for a story, or if a group of children have been busy exploring, investigating and finding out something, this could be an opportunity to send a message as a surprise! Duplicate messages could be sent to more than one parent, for example 'Wow! What a fun packed morning we have had, ask me all about our Pirate Ship when you pick me up!'

Sending messages to all parents could be really useful at times, especially if there is urgency to the message, for example: 'We are closed today due to...', 'The photographer is visiting tomorrow morning — remember a clean jumper and big smile!'

Using a text messaging service could be a useful way to reach parents who may not always bring their child to or from nursery but are still keen to keep up-to-date with events and news. Taking up the offer of a free trial of a text messaging service would enable settings to see if the method could work for them and also provide an opportunity to seek parents' views of the service.

## Valuing diversity

By talking to the parents in your setting you will get to know their interests and skills. By valuing the diversity and mix of families you are teaching the children in your setting an awareness of their community. There could be parents who would be happy to share their particular skills or hobbies. Through shared communication, you may also be able to support vulnerable families within the community. Invite local vets, dentists, florists, lorry drivers, police officers or estate agents to share their expertise and skills. Any roles that your parents play in the community will be of interest to the children.

Above all else, home learning should be about spending quality time together as a family.

*'Let children be children. A skilled five year old grows from a busy four year old, a curious three year old, a cuddled two year old, an adventurous one year old and a communicative baby.'*

**http://www.early-education.uk**

## References

Perry, B. D (2002) *Childhood Experience and the Expression of Genetic Potential; What Childhood Neglect Tells Us About Nature and Nurture.*

Sue Palmer (2006) *Toxic Childhood – How the Modern World is Damaging Our Children and What We Can Do about It.*

Web sites:

www.earlyhomelearning.org.uk

http://www.early-education.uk

# Chapter 7
# Case Study: Sandcastles Playgroup

Each and every setting is unique, individual and bursting with wonderful ideas. Sharing ideas and visiting other settings can be an invaluable opportunity to see ideas in practice and maybe inspire your own practice.

Here we take a more detailed look at how Sandcastles Playgroup in Suffolk works in partnership with parents. Sandcastles Playgroup caters for children between the ages of 3-5 Years.

## Establishing a partnership

Sandcastles Playgroup strives to find out as much as possible about each child and their family. Before a child begins at Sandcastles their parent/carer is encouraged to make several visits together with the child (as many visits as they wish) on any day at any time. These visits enable children and parents to become familiar with the environment, staff, other children and the types of everyday occurrences such as, the snack bar, storytime or Tilly the pet tortoise!

These visits prove highly valuable for staff to begin to get to know new children and their families, whilst also being crucial for easing any worries or anxieties the parents or children might have. Instantly, children and their parent have a shared joint understanding of what their playgroup is about and what types of things happen there – just perfect for chatting about at home! Allowing parents to visit at anytime or on any day, demonstrates the open, transparent and supportive approach to working together in partnership.

Together, staff discuss with parents their individual child, this provides a wonderful opportunity for recording information about each child in an 'All About Me' booklet or box (described on page 70). Sandcastles always complete any forms or information booklets together with parents, as the leader explained:

*'Parents always say so much more when we chat, more than they ever put on any forms. It's hard for parents who may have questions about any information needed and they are at home trying to fill it in on their own, often late at night when the children have gone to bed. We always chat about information together, whether it is a transition form as the children move to school, a care plan or finding out about individual children when they first join. We find out so much during these chats that is so useful for us, the parent and ultimately the child'.*

The information gathered from parents is then used to plan the learning environment, activities and resources based on the interests and preferences of their child. Staff, particularly Key Workers, have an insight into the child and can use this as a starting point for getting to know them.

## Parent feedback

Sandcastles provides a comprehensive information pack for parents, designed to give as much information as possible about their child's new playgroup, including policies and procedures (all in jargon free easy reading format), the history of the playgroup, aims, values, who's who and what they can expect from the playgroup. A great deal of thought has been given to the accessibility of this information. It contains a wealth of information, in a simple easy-to-read layout, with photographs and examples, along with signposting for finding out more. This information is not simply passed on and then forgotten about. Staff at Sandcastles seek feedback from parents to ensure that they are providing relevant and useful information.

As a result of parent feedback, changes are often made. For example, parents commented that a list of staff names would be helpful as it was difficult to match faces to names, especially as not all staff worked every session. In response to this, photographs of each member of staff were included with staff details in the information pack, along with large photos of 'Staff Working This Session…' by the entrance doors.

Regular information sessions are held covering all aspects of the setting's work and development. The times of these sessions are sensitively planned to cater for a wide range of parents' commitments, with sessions available during the day or evening. Refreshments are always provided and an opportunity to chat.

## The little things

It is the well thought out little things that make such a big difference:

### Location of children's coat pegs

*The children's coat pegs are located in the messy, creative area at the far end of the room. There is space near to the door where parents and children come in but as the leader explained,*

'We want the parents to be a part of each day, to feel welcome, included and part of our playgroup. By putting the pegs at the end of the room, parents have to physically come through. They often share little gems of information as they walk through such as, 'She tried mango for the first time last night' or 'We've all got a cold'. They can see all of the things we have been doing, photographs and information on display.'

This also adds to the relaxed, flowing feel at the beginning and end of each session where:

- parents see other parents and have an opportunity to get to know one another

- children can share their playgroup with their parents, perhaps showing them who their friends are, the model they created or the story they shared that day

- key workers can informally share how children have been spending their time and celebrate their achievements, as well as keeping them informed of upcoming events

- younger siblings feel part of the playgroup and older siblings attending playgroup are supported to chat to staff about their life at home, 'We're now going to Tesco in our red car!'

- new staff or students can observe firsthand how to interact with parents in a warm, friendly and professional manner.

## Personal letters

*An individual letter and accompanying personal statement from a child's key worker is sent to each child and their parent when they start.*

The letter introduces the need and importance of a key worker, it encourages and welcomes input from parents and highlights how this really helps to build up a full picture of their child, it also shares the days and sessions which they work.

The key worker's personal statement shares details about themselves, their family and their interests along with their qualifications, experience and any recent training.

This is a perfect way for parents and children to relate to their key worker — common interests are often found, such as, 'Wow! Debbie has a dog too!' and 'We always go to Cornwall on holiday'. It helps to build a relationship, knowing a little more personal and professional detail of a child's key worker.

## Puppets going home!

Sandcastles has a selection of large puppets, all of which are named and an integral part of daily life at Sandcastles. The puppets love going home to play with the children! They each have their own little kit ready for a weekend of fun, wherever that may be! Parents and children can write messages, attach photographs or choose any other way to share what the puppets have been up to. This has proved really useful in finding out more about children's lives at home, particularly those who might spend the weekend with a parent who does not often bring them to playgroup.

Towards the end of each year, the different puppets begin to wear uniforms from the schools which the children will be moving on to. When the children visit and move to their new school, the familiar puppet, complete with uniform, will be waiting for them there.

## Maintaining partnerships – every step of the way

Sandcastles Playgroup values and respects the partnerships it has with parents. It actively seeks to build upon and maintain these partnerships, reviewing and altering its approaches to meet the needs of different and new groups of parents and children.

Detailed below are just some of the events or activities that have recently taken place or are planned for the near future.

### Family days out

A family trip to a local attraction: this year at Duxford Imperial War Museum — a chance to see aeroplanes up close and even go on Concord! Wherever possible the trips take into account interests of the children. Coaches are provided to ensure that the whole family can enjoy a day out with the playgroup.

Sandcastles staff found that by organising a family trip it gave everyone an opportunity to meet other families. This has been really beneficial for families new to the area.

Often, as a result of these trips, parents then arrange to meet up again at the local park or play area. All staff attend the family trips and use the opportunity to chat and interact with parents and children in an exciting and new environment as well as supporting families wherever needed, for example, by looking after twin babies or helping to push a wheelchair.

## Lively and multi-sensory workshops

Parents are invited to workshops to find out more about specific areas of learning and development. These are designed to help parents discover more about the relationship between playing and learning, what happens at playgroup and how they can support their child at home. Workshops are a chance for parents to share what they do at home, ask any questions and share their successes or concerns. Very often it is the parent's questions or comments which determine the focus of further workshops. A recent workshop focussing on early language development, invited parents to participate in a wide variety of language rich, multi-sensory activities. Staff were able to model and discuss with parents the learning and development that each activity could promote.

Ideas for supporting children at home are realistic and respectful of parent's busy lives and the demands of young children! Chatting about daily events in an open and honest manner can be really supportive for parents. Here's just one example: At a recent workshop the leader explained that discussing a story at bedtime could be a wonderful opportunity to enhance language development (and many other things) as she was all too aware that parents very often could be thinking 'Quick, let's get through this book so I can go downstairs for Eastenders or to wash up or I need to have a cup of tea and grown up time!' Many parents completely related to this! Giving an opportunity to share ideas about the quality of the talk during storytime and to reassure parents it's ok to spend twenty minutes talking about one picture or follow children's ideas, 'If I was Little Red Riding Hood I would...'. Stories didn't have to be raced through to get the end; children need time and a chance to talk about their ideas, as well as listening to a story, without heading for a very lengthy bedtime story. Parents were reassured to hear that quality over quantity was important!

Parents reported that they felt reassured that by involving their child in everyday occurrences (as shared by Sandcastles staff) such as, counting the steps as they go up any stairs, allowing them to chop the mushrooms for tea, having their own little cloth for cleaning the sink or bath, was enough for supporting their learning and that they didn't need to sit down and look at numbers or letters every day.

## Involving parents in fun professional development

An innovative approach to involving parents in some aspects of Sandcastles professional development is currently being planned. A popular and well known storyteller and ex-school inspector has been booked to work with the setting, covering every angle by spending the day storytelling with children, then holding a storytelling workshop for staff (local schools invited too) and finishing with 'An Evening with....' for parents.

Understanding the needs of families, an evening session is planned with a crèche for children, along with refreshments and nibbles. Staff are really hoping for a fun, relaxed, sociable, evening rich with inspiration and ideas.

## Open sessions for parents

Parents are able to come and help or spend the session at playgroup whenever they choose. During specific weeks all parents are also offered the opportunity to sign up for an half an hour session with their child's key worker, outside of session times. Offering parents a range of times up until about 8pm in the evening gives all parents, particularly working parents, flexibility to be able to attend. Together at these sessions, parents and their child's key worker chat about things the child enjoys at playgroup, home, their individual development, preferences and patterns of behaviour, whilst having the opportunity to share their learning journey — detailing their achievements and development over a period of time.

Again, parents' feedback is always sought with a questionnaire seeking their views, for example: Was the session long enough, were the times suitable, did anything surprise you? The feedback that practitioners get from such questions allows them to plan future open sessions based on the needs and wishes of parents.

Capturing parents' thoughts in a comments book, together with questionnaires, helps support Sandcastles' self-evaluation. By having a 'big parent presence' at the beginning and end of each session, it is easier to give reminders of times and days of their session, and it clearly works with 69 out of 73 parents attending the last open session.

Lovely seeing Rey's work and progress. Nice to see how well Rey has settled in and how much he enjoys being here. Rey loves coming to Sandcastles and is always talking about his special ladies.

Many thanks

Penny (Rey's mum)

# Valuing parents' information sharing

Sandcastles has many children who have English as an Additional Language. Parents instantly feel included through a vibrant multilingual environment, translated information and quality one-to-one time with staff who share observations, very often through photographs, of how their child spends their time at playgroup. One parent has written key words and phrases in their home language and given these to staff should their child become upset or distressed whilst they are away. These are on display close to a cosy area so staff can instantly access them when they may be in the area with the child.

One of the parents recently shared how her son really loved electrical items and was intrigued how they worked. Staff used this information as an opportunity to build on his interests and engage him through providing old electrical items (one being an answering machine) and screwdrivers and tools to take them apart. The excitement, learning and communication, both verbal and non-verbal, during the experience was described as powerful for both child and practitioner and was just the beginning of a series of learning experiences and opportunities based on one child's interests.

With Fathers Day approaching, staff were capturing children's responses to 'Can you tell me about your daddy' using a dictaphone. Children were then involved in transferring their recording onto a laptop and then a CD. The discussions that emerged were individual to each child and their family. One child was intrigued about how it would get to his daddy as he lived in America...

Families clearly appreciate the individual touches, thought and dedication that Sandcastles give to each and every family.

It is hoped that this case study will provide a snapshot of some of the ways a playgroup setting engages and works in partnership with parents. Their approach is tailored to their individual families, community and location. Much of their success can be attributed to their clearly visible attitude to flexibility which was apparent across the setting.

The young child dressed as a (very!) large shark during Storytime or the child who, during a carpet session, wandered over to the painting area to look for a previously created model to add a little more detail to it; these demonstrate the aspirations of the setting as the leader describes:

*'We respect the individuality of the children. We want them to be happy and content with who they are in later life. We enjoy learning from them, watching them becoming people, confident and happy with themselves.'*

There are no 'getting ready' for school activities by age inappropriate tasks. The children are all busy, engrossed and engaged in who they are now, absorbed in discovering and learning. Through individual schemas and interests their characters and personalities are allowed to shine and blossom.

Maintaining a continuous partnership between home and school, long after initial transition and settling activities, is hugely important in a young child's life. An open, honest and transparent partnership built on trust, respect and honesty, where information and approaches from home and school complement one another, offer a great opportunity to build on a child's experiences at home or school and really impact on learning and development.

*'Parents and practitioners have a lot to learn from each other. This can help them to support and extend children's learning and development.'*

EYFS, (2008)

Chapter 8

Case Study: Sproughton Primary School

Individual schools have their own individual, adaptable and successful approaches to maintaining regular and purposeful two-way communication between home and school.

Here we look at some of the approaches undertaken by Sproughton Primary School, located in Ipswich, Suffolk.

From the first glance children's home lives have a visible presence in school, as seen through an eye catching, 'Wow Tree'. This 3D tree has children's photos, drawings and mark making, all from home, hanging from it.

As their teacher Kathryn explained, 'The children love bringing in photographs or things they have made at home, they especially love pegging them onto the tree. It has turned into a real conversation hub, children chat to one another about their items, and it's lovely to hear them talk about family members in photographs or describing how they made their sparkly creations!'

## Parental involvement

The school runs weekly parent sessions, where parents are invited into the school to have an active role in their child's learning. Parents are able to join their child for a morning each week. During this time they may be involved in number adventures, reading activities or messy fun, to name just a few examples. Parents have reported that it really helps to see firsthand what their child does in school. The scheduled weekly morning session has been designed to enable parents to have the opportunity to meet other parents. Children's individual records of learning are displayed and available for parents to view and feed their information into.

At Sproughton Primary there are many items transferring backwards and forwards between school and home. Sending home a teddy bear with a diary is by no means a new idea. However, Sproughton has taken a slightly different approach to this idea, which has proved very popular with both children and parents:

Children decide upon pretend pets at the start of each year. These pets are then equipped with their own, jointly sourced, accessories, e.g. a pet carrier, food bowl and lead. Each pet has its own diary too. The 'class pets' go home with children on a flexible basis. Children love filling in each pet's diary with drawings, photographs, tickets, in fact anything that represents what the pets have been doing with them at home.

Allowing children to choose the type of pet to go home and spend time with them has resulted in some interesting findings! For example, dragon's diary and tales were far more imaginative and quirkier than the adventures of the more traditional pets such as a dog or hamster.

As the personal lives and interests of the children are shared through the adventures of the creatures, on an almost daily basis, the learning environment can easily be adapted to reflect children's recent experiences and activities. Conversations independently flowed as children found common interests in their personal lives 'I've been to that zoo!' 'My garden has a goalpost too'.

## Our Little Books!

It's not just pretend pets that go backwards and forwards between school and homes. Regular communication about children's time at school is shared in their home environment through exciting Little Books!

'Our Little Books' are designed to promote discussion between children and their parents, using the starting point of activities or events that children have been engaged in at school.

The Little Books that the current class of Reception children and their teacher have created include:

- Our Little Book of Imaginative Learning

- Our Little Book of Outdoor Learning

- Our Little Book of Everyday Learning

- Our Little Book of Creative Learning

- Our Little Wedding Book

- Our Little Circus Book

Our Little Books are full of photographs, children's mark making, drawings and information about all the things the children have been learning, discovering and finding out about. As well as promoting talk, these Little Books give parents a great insight into how their child spends their time at school and provide a base of information that can be built upon and enhanced by experiences at home.

The Little Books cover specific themes, such as weddings or the circus, and more general areas such as 'imaginative learning'. The quotes in the books are from children and practitioners and paint a picture of the learning journey, i.e. they highlight the development and learning that was evident during their investigations.

The idea of Our Little Books is not solely limited to the books being sent from school to home. After several parent workshops, some of which focussed on the value and language of play and how to

support children's play and learning at home, it was felt that a book to capture a snapshot of children's play and learning in their home environment would be hugely beneficial in supporting children's learning at school.

The information which comes into school via 'My Little Book of the Wonderful Learning I Do at Home' has been exceptionally informative in helping to plan for children's learning at school. For example one parent had shared via the book that 'Whilst watching a film on Saturday, Theo noticed that the dragon had three eyes on one side of his face. He told me that the dragon had 6 eyes because he had three on each side of his face and three and three make six'. This information was hugely valuable for Kathryn the class teacher who over the past few weeks had been teaching and playing with pairs of numbers. It confirmed Theo's understanding and ability to transfer his knowledge into different contexts at both school and home.

Clearly, a huge focus is placed on stimulating talk and discussion between children and their parents. The school actively offers parents many 'ways in' to chat with their child and find out more about their explorations and learning at school.

# Time to talk

The focus on promoting talk to support children's learning is reinforced with a weekly 'Time to talk' activity which reinforces children's discoveries and learning within school. Parents are given a picture or thought bubble with often one or two open ended questions, such as, 'What can you tell me about The Three Little Pigs?' or 'Why do we have puddles?' In this simple way parents are able to gain a snapshot of some of the things their child has been busy finding out about at school. One parent commented 'I am just amazed at how much she knows. We learn all sorts of new things and it often leads to us using the internet or asking family members to help us with all the new questions that come out!'

A very popular member of the class is Talk Time Wolf, who leisurely sits in his deckchair in the classroom and loves to listen to children's stories, tales and adventures from home. Either in small groups or on an individual basis, children enjoy sharing their home life with Talk Time Wolf.

## Fun sessions!

Parents are an integral part of school life and many events are planned to enable parents to share in their child's learning, whilst demonstrating and sharing their own skills too.

A recent focus on the theme of 'The Circus' ended on a high, with parents coming in at the end of the week to join the children for a circus skills session! An entertaining and relaxed session took place where parents and children were able to laugh and learn together!

Just like every setting, not all parents are able to attend events during the school day. Careful consideration is given to holding events and sessions at times out of the school day, giving all parents equal opportunity to work in partnership and be involved in their child's life at school, as much as possible.

Teachers are very mindful that when children and their parents begin school, they can have their own pre-conceived ideas, which are often linked to their own fears

and experiences of school or the school environment. Frequent workshops for parents, designed to breakdown the 'language' of school and demonstrate what the reality of phonics or numeracy looks like in practice, helps to alleviate some parents' apprehensions and show how children, parents and practitioners can enjoy discovering and learning together.

Successful relationships between parents and educators can have long-lasting and beneficial effects on children's learning and well-being.

*'Successful relationships become partnerships, when there is two-way communication and parents and practitioners really listen to each other and value each other's views and support in achieving the best outcomes for each child.'*

EYFS (2008)

# Staying together

# Ensuring ongoing successful partnerships

Working in partnership with parents is a continuous, evolving cycle. It is part of daily life in all settings. No one-off event or workshop is enough to think that the 'parent partnership box' can be ticked.

Each and every family is unique and what suits and works for one family, might well be a non-working option for another family. Just as children need a wide range of experiences and activities to suit their individual needs, parents also need a wide range of options for working together in partnership.

Valuing and respecting the diversity of families, their working patterns and lifestyles is essential in ensuring that both parents and child feel welcomed, valued and an equal partner.

Establishing together from the beginning, the importance and vast development opportunities behind everyday occurrences, such as outdoor learning, book sharing, cooking or 'firsthand experiences', can help parents and practitioners to begin to build partnerships, on mutual understanding of the purpose and value of daily experiences.

It is from here that partnerships can develop as key workers get to know each child, sharing and comparing with parents their observations and expertise of their child at home. Together you can plan the next steps for learning.

Parents have a right to find out more, to understand their child's development and in turn how they can support their play and learning.

*'An attitude towards parents whereby teachers and other educators are prepared to think about and articulate their own pedagogy and to discuss it with parents and the wider community is now essential in the development of effective early education.'*

Nutbrown, C. (2011)

Sharing with parents the fascinating world behind children's patterns of behaviour and exploring schemas can be enlightening. It can form the basis of discussions about children's behaviour patterns at home and school.

*'Teachers who have shared their interest in schemas and talked with parents about the ways in which they use this theory to support children's development have often found that parents become more interested in this way of looking at and making sense of children's actions, their talk and their mark making.'*

Nutbrown, C. (2011)

One practitioner vividly remembers the impact of sharing ideas about schemas with a group of parents. Initially using images and video clips of the children engaged in play, some of the examples showed children pushing buggies, riding bikes, spinning ribbons, sitting in boxes, jumping off milk crates, swinging small brooms and filling cake cases with wet and dry sand. Parents began to share some of their own observations about their children's behaviour at home, causing much laughter and many similarities between the children. The similarities provided the perfect opportunity to discuss patterns of behaviour and schemas. Parents were amazed! And asked many questions to help them try to 'sort' their children's behaviour into schemas. It gave reassurance to many parents as they began to understand, 'Oh that's why he has to throw everything about the house!' And 'No wonder I keep finding all the beads wrapped up!'

Together we looked at and discussed ideas of how children's schemas can be supported and their behaviour and fascinations explored. The following week after the meeting a parent rushed in, desperate to share her news and ask what to do! Aisha's mum explained:

*'I watched Aisha play for ages; she drew a picture for Daddy, just a small picture. Then she put it in an envelope, then into a sandwich bag, then into a carrier bag, then she found one of my shopping bags and put it in there and then she put it in the cupboard under the stairs! I was amazed - I could see it was the 'insidey' thing that we were talking about the other night. What else could I give her? I'm going to chat to Saffron's mum because I remember laughing when she told me she liked to put things inside the washing machine and shoes – I'm going to see what else she does!'*

This exchange of information and request for ideas was the beginning of many discussions about Aisha's patterns of behaviour. Over the coming weeks and months Russian dolls, stacking boxes, envelopes, bags (from money bags to huge holdalls), lifts in shopping centres and stories with an enclosure link were just some of the resources and activities used to support Aisha's investigations. It was the start of many discussions, most of them informal, about how Aisha was enjoying and experimenting with enveloping across different areas of the setting and home.

Together, through a more formal planned meeting, individual (and quieter!) time was given to reviewing observations (many of which involved animals in cages and boxes in the vets role play area!) and comparing Aisha's learning and development at home and school. From here, together, we were able to identify and plan her next steps in learning and discuss ideas of how we could each support this at home and school.

Involving both children and parents in reflecting on children's experiences and achievements promotes positivity, self-esteem and a love of learning. Aisha was in control of her learning, she was

facilitated by her practitioners and parents observing, talking with and listening to her and responding with resources and experiences to support her pattern of thinking.

Quality time to talk is an important and integral element of effective partnerships. This is when you have a chance to review and reflect upon the child's time within the setting, share their experiences, discuss their interests, patterns of behaviour and find out more about the child out of the setting. It is an opportunity to plan the next steps, activities and experiences tailored for individual children's learning needs.

## Quick tips

A quick tips board near to where parents may enter the building or a little star shaped paper with one tip written on could help parents with a quick suggestion of something to try at home, this could easily become a two way process as practitioners encourage parents to share their tips. Here are some examples:

### Quick tips – linked to schemas

- Give your child some empty bottles, sprays and pumps in the bath. Watch what they do! Do you notice anything? Please come and share with your child's key worker.

### Quick tips – general home ideas

- Count how many shoes are by your door. Ask your child to match up the pairs. Demonstrate counting the shoes in twos.

### Quick tips – linked to a theme

- This week has been full of dentist fun! Can you see any pictures of teeth on signs, posters, shops, buses or in magazines? Whose teeth are they? I wonder why they are there...? We can't wait to hear of any places you may see pictures of teeth!

Communicating with parents, carers and families will be very different for each individual setting. Consistently reviewing and reflecting upon your approach to working with parents will ensure that your setting is actively seeking to establish, develop and maintain a positive, purposeful partnership – with the child at the centre.

### References

Nutbrown, C. (2011) *Threads of Thinking*, SAGE Publications, London

PEAL – Parents, Early Years and Learning — offers training and resources to support working with parents. www.peal.org.uk

Having considered the importance of working with parents in your setting, inevitably, there will come a time when the children move on from your care and you no longer have the regular contact with those parents. For many parents transition time can be a time of worry. As they have grown to trust and respect the practitioners working with their child, those practitioners will no longer be part of their daily care and so new relationships and partnerships will need to be forged.

The important issue of transition is explored in detail in many publications. The following two books provide essential reading for practitioners looking for in-depth guidance and ideas for managing and creating smooth transitions between Reception and Year One.

## Further reading:

Featherstone, S. (2009) *Making it Work in Year One*, Featherstone Education, Bloomsbury Publishing plc

Bayley, R. & Featherstone, S. (2009) *Smooth Transitions*, Featherstone Education, Bloomsbury Publishing plc

Just a fraction of working with parents at times of transition is explored below.

Transition times cover a variety of periods of change in a child's educational journey. In the early years these can include from home to pre-school/nursery, from pre-school/nursery to school and from Reception into KS1.

These periods provide a point in time where practitioners can reinforce their relationship with parents. By getting to know the new set of children and families, practitioners are better prepared to develop the unique child entering their setting.

Planning for transition is vital and time and energy should be spent making sure it is a cyclical all year event, rather than within the last 2 or 3 weeks.

*'The process of transfer takes time, over time. Activities take place at different points and over different periods'*

**Featherstone, S. (2009)**

For practitioners one of the most valuable resources that you have to use is your previous cohort's parent group. Ask them to evaluate your practice through a questionnaire sent home to past parents about things they enjoyed, things they loved, and things that could be improved upon.

Essentials for new parents should include:

- Making sure that parents are involved from the beginning, when they make their first initial enquiry.

- Ensuring that parents are well informed months before term starts and any initial worries or concerns are discussed and shared.

- Sharing your aspirations for a 'settling time' in the early weeks and months and for parents to be welcomed and actively involved.

- Making sure parents know their contributions are valued, very much sought and essential for their child's learning.

- Communicating in a variety of ways to make sure all parents know term dates, uniform expectations, times of sessions, names of staff (through use of photos), where to hang coats and where the toilets are.

Some other ideas for consideration:

- Providing photos of the staff will help the child and their families know who their teachers are and will help when they have a friendly face they can relate to on their first day.

- Hosting pop in sessions before, after or during school for parents and children to visit the setting together in the weeks and months before they join.

- Practitioners writing a personal letter to the child and their family with a friendly welcome and some information about themselves.

- Initiating a summer or weekend picnic at a local park or similar venue for families and children to attend - a neutral place to come together and talk and get to know one another. This allows practitioners to talk to parents informally and gives opportunity to identify and ease any worries or concerns parents may have.

For children who are already established in a setting and are moving up to a new group or class the same respect should be given, providing full communication and ensuring parents and children are prepared. Allowing children currently in your setting time to make regular visits to their new area and then following through with the opportunity to talk with their current familiar adult about what they have seen can help to ease worries.

Children's new practitioner(s) will need ample opportunity to observe children in their current environment, with familiar adults, resources and routines. Ensuring that children's new practitioner(s) have had an opportunity to meet the parents prior to starting, will be the first step in forging new partnerships.

Parents too will need the opportunity to visit the new learning environment and familiarise themselves with the location of pegs, toilets, noticeboards and entrance and exit details.

Communicating clearly with parents and making sure that they always know when their child has visited or been visited by their new practitioner will ensure that parents have the chance to chat and discuss the visits with their child. Children should be encouraged to share their thoughts and experiences and voice any worries or concerns.

## Observation visits

Practitioners should try to observe the children who will be joining them whilst they are in their current learning environment so that they can gain an understanding of the routines and expectations and have a valuable chance to see children engaged in play with familiar resources and friends. After the long summer holidays and the change in routine, children may well change so a visit to see children in their current setting is very worthwhile.

Many school processes will be very alien to children, and many children will never have had a tray, a peg, or a book bag to contend with. It is vital that you take time to show children where to go and what to do and which adults are available to help them.

Make time for both practitioners (old and new) to meet to discuss children — their individuality and passions whilst sharing learning journey information and EYFS profile details.

Transfer information should be concise and useful. Developing planning and provision in the Autumn Term, to allow for a play based learning environment, will be essential.

*'Everything we now know tells us that a 'bottom up' model, where the best of Foundation Stage practice is extended into Year 1 is more likely to be successful than over preparation of children in a 'top down' model which puts inappropriate pressure on children in Reception.'*

**Bayley, R. et al. (2009)**

Having the chance to visit children in their current setting, be it at a childminders, pre-school or nursery, before they join you provides the chance to: Leave book bags, sweatshirts and photographic books all about their new setting.

This will allow children to play with the items in an environment that is safe and secure to them. Children can show their parents the items in their dressing up or role play area and share with them photographic books of their new setting.

> Watch how children interact with familiar peers, which areas they prefer and routines they are used to – What happens at tidy up time? Are particular words or resources used? Practitioners can then mirror an element in their setting ready for when children transition through. A familiar role play area or dinosaur small world could be a source of comfort to a child in a new and strange environment.

Making 'time to talk' to new parents, whether during a home visit or individual time at your setting will be valuable for beginning to develop an understanding of each child and their family.

As children move up into KS1, early years practitioners should ensure as much as possible that early years principles and practices remain:

- Spend less time sitting still.

- Plan for firsthand experiences and exploration of materials.

- Promote physical control.

- Allow children to follow through an idea with sufficient time.

- Rehearse and develop ideas on a range of expressive 2-and 3-dimensional media.

- Experience play-based activities e.g. sand, water, role-play, construction, outdoors.

- Engage in imaginative play, music and dance.

- Communicate through free-ranging talking with peers and adults.

- Learn within an appropriate environment indoors and outdoors.

- Promote observation-led assessment.

- Involve children with making the classroom their own, e.g. making displays and labels.

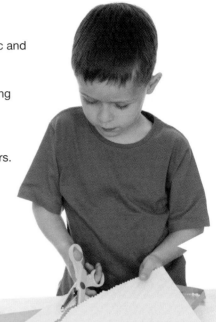

## 'All About Me' boxes at transition time

Ask parents and children to create an 'All About Me' box, by filling a box with pictures of family, pets, favourite toys, memories and special messages from home. Making the boxes provides parents with a chance to celebrate how special their child is. It allows time for love and security and discussion. Upon arrival at their new setting the boxes provide a wonderful talking point for child and practitioner and enable practitioners to instantly gain an understanding of each child. Allow time and resources for parents and children to make the boxes!

# Home visits

Make time, wherever possible, to carry out a home visit. (If this is not possible make time for a setting visit.) During the home visit, put the family at ease by telling them that you are there to get to know their child and not to make any judgements on their housework! Take question prompts to keep you on track and find out all of the things that are important to the child and family. What do they love doing? Are they frightened of anything? Who is important to them? What are their pets or cuddly toys called?

Remembering personal information will instantly calm a worried child during their first few days. It is amazing the things that will stick in your head after a visit with a family. If you can ask about their summer camping trip and did they remember to take Jess the dog… you will have awarded yourself big brownie points in the child's eyes. They will seem important to you, and therefore confirm to the child that they are important and valued.

It is a nice gesture to provide children with a special key ring or token relevant to your setting, the key ring or token can then be used to attach special photographs (perhaps of special people, family, home, toys, memories or pets). The key ring and photos are then brought into the setting and are a constant secure reminder of home.

A child moving setting can be very unsettling and hugely damaging if not handled correctly. To ensure that each child is happy and confident take time to make every person feel welcome and important to you.

*'May they all move forward with their enthusiasm maintained, their wonder increased and their self esteem intact.'*

Featherstone, S. (2009)

### References

Featherstone, S. (2009) *Making it Work in Year One*, Featherstone Education, Bloomsbury Publishing plc

Bayley,R. & Featherstone, S. (2009) *Smooth Transitions*, Featherstone Education, Bloomsbury Publishing plc

# References and useful information

Bayley, R. & Featherstone, S. (2009) *Smooth Transitions*, Featherstone Education, Bloomsbury Publishing plc

Department for Children, Schools and Families (DCSF) (2008) *Statutory Framework for the Early Years Foundation Stage*. Nottingham: HMSO

Dowling, M. (2010) *Young Children's Personal, Social & Emotional Development*, SAGE Publications

Edwards, C., Gandini, L., & Forman, G. (1993) *The Hundred Languages of Children, The Reggio Emilia Approach to Early Childhood Education*, Ablex Publishing Corporation

Einarsdottir, J and Wagner, J (2005) *Nordic Childhoods and Early Education*, Information Age Publishing

Featherstone, S. (2009) *Making it Work in Year One*, Featherstone Education, Bloomsbury Publishing plc

Gerhardt, S. (2010) *Why Love Matters,* Routledge Publishers

Goleman, D. (1996) *Emotional Intelligence: Why it can matter more than IQ*, Bloomsbury Publishing plc

Hannaford, C. (1995) *Why learning is not all in your head*, Great Ocean Publishers

NCSL (2011) *Leadership for Parental Engagement*

Nutbrown, C. (2011) *Threads of Thinking*, SAGE Publications

Perry, Bruce (2002) *Childhood Experience and the Expression of Genetic Potential; What Childhood Neglect Tells Us About Nature and Nurture,* Klumer Academic Publishers

Sunderland, M. (2007) *What every parent needs to know (The Science of Parenting)* DK

Te Whāriki: *New Zealand's Early Childhood Curriculum Document in Theory and Practice*. Wellington: New Zealand Council for Education Research

Tickell, C. (2011) *Independent report on: The Early Years: Foundations for life, health and learning*

Thornton. L and Brunton, P (2007) *Bringing the Reggio Approach to your Early Years Practice*. Routledge Publishers

## Bibliography

Bruner, J. (1990) *Acts of Meaning*, Harvard University Press.

Bruner, J. (1996). *The Culture of Education*. Cambridge, MA: Harvard University Press.

Dixon, P. (2005) *Let Me Be* Peche Luna

Donaldson, M. (1983) *Children's Mind,* Fontana/Collins.

Gordon, M (2009) *Roots of Empathy,* Thomas Allen Publishers

Harpin, L (2009) *Promising Partnerships*. Rowman and Littlefield Education Publishers

Holt, J. (1991) *How Children Learn*, Penguin

Louv, R (2010) *Last Child in the Woods,* Atlantic Books

Wheeler, H and Connor, J (2009) *Parents, Early Years and Learning*. National Children's Bureau

## Websites

**www.earlyhomelearning.org**

**www.minedu.govt.nz -**
Final report to the Ministry of Education. Wellington: New Zealand Council for Educational Research.

**www.early-education.uk**

**www.peal.org.uk**
PEAL (Parents, Early Years and Learning) offers training and resources to support working with parents.